CAKE

CAKE

JEN ROUSE

HEADMISTRESS PRESS

ISBN 978-0-9995930-4-2

Cover art by Hilma af Klint, *Primordial Chaos, No. 24, Group I* (1906-
1907). Public Domain.
Cover & book design by Mary Meriam.

PUBLISHER
Headmistress Press
60 Shipview Lane
Sequim, WA 98382
Telephone: 917-428-8312
Email: headmistresspress@gmail.com
Website: headmistresspress.blogspot.com

CAKE
is dedicated to those who pay
a remarkable kind of attention.

CONTENTS

Hummingbird Girl Gets Married   1

Approaching   2

The Failed Abduction of Hummingbird Girl   4

Aurora Borealis   5

When She Sings   6

An Afternoon in Paris   7

Whatever These Ruins   9

Call Her Name   11

Remedy   12

Heavenly   14

A Remarkable Kind of Attention   16

Chrysopoeia   20

And These, My Least Best Selves   22

Resurrection   25

Petite Rouge   27

Additional Duties as Required   29

Cake   30

About the Author   33

Acknowlegments   35

HUMMINGBIRD GIRL GETS MARRIED

Vows flew around her
in holy moth orbit.
Her prayer hands
held a secret and
her veil—well,
nothing much. Just
her hummingbird
head, silky as
a wedding dress, which
she was wearing,
by the way. It seemed
so white and uneventful.
Not like the circling
moths, not
like the holes
in the light. And the phantom
skirt on the floor.

Do you take this skirt
and these hands,
maybe these moths,
wholly to be
embraced in a bouquet
of pink peonies?

Do you take
this cake,
hypnotic and
towering,
humming
in bird-wedding
delight?

APPROACHING

And so she flew in

with the loveliest cake,

a bird-shaped head,

scarlet as a hummingbird's

throat. Bird humming

happily. She has made

the thickest most

luscious cake like

a low-throated song,

nectar of orange

blossoms—and she

licked my fingers.

No, I licked my fingers.

Hers.

Why haven't you come

through the waves

in so long? I sighed.

She should have

smelled like orange

blossoms and honey.

How she flew in

with the cake—and her

delicious arms were gasping

branches, honey-sapped,

with small scarlet

nonpareils. "Gertrude

Stein," she hummed like

a tiny bird, "she baked

this birthday cake for you."

This cake. One cake.

Will you offer it

to the birds?

THE FAILED ABDUCTION OF HUMMINGBIRD GIRL

The year they came
for her, in their
cloistered thinking, with
their alien-inspired
goo rays, the Saturn version,
of course—she had already
been preparing. At
the door they hissed
and patted goo bellies.
She had never believed
in them really, having
only seen them in germs,
returned items, and
lint traps.

A week before,
she had said, "Head, I sense,
we are to part. But
only for a short interlude."
And Hummingbird folded
herself like an accordion.
It was a sight.

Her sister packed her carefully
in layers of tissue, and
between each layer, jam.
Lick-your-fingers good.
Cause a girl has to eat.
It was a steamer trunk
of a cake. And when she
rose like the rabbit god,
and shook her tail
feather, they never
knew what hit them.

Aurora Borealis

When it's all too much,
she flies north, to pine
and cedar and a lonely
fawn. They dance
like lovers, like druids
at midnight. Sucking
breath from the fathoms
of what has been forgotten.
She wears her sequined head
and, her fawn, the horn
of an ancient unicorn. *Come
close,* she whispers. *Why don't you
call anymore? Where
have you been?*

Fawn, in a field of poppies:
*There are whole years
of sleep and dreams
that reek of you. Your
demands that I speak
spark the sky, and
I would leap so far
to touch you—but you
only ask when your
own heart hurts.*

And so she turns
and licks the trees,
shakes her soft-
feathered head
and hums like fire
through a fountain
of night sky.

WHEN SHE SINGS

She is quick to store
every sticky word to her tongue—
a repertoire so rich
one would get the sugar shakes
from it, and to be touched
by her, even once,
with her vocal chords
all a flutter in your head,
careening and crooning
that lullaby you imagine
her laying down beside you with, it
feels like being on Saturn,
swimming in candy rings,
licking your quick fingers,
brushing her cheek
to flame. That's the way
you have to love her:
with a fleeting aria,
with your entire being.

AN AFTERNOON IN PARIS

Of course we should all
kick up our heels and
run through historic fountains—
Parisian, preferably.
And we are smiling in
our cotton-candy
dresses. Our reflections
flickering
like fin-glistening
koi. Fists clenching
cake.

Over there
a silver-
haired mermaid
on a bicycle. She circles
and circles, moonlight
in the spokes
of her laughter.

These streets
are cobbled
with mirth, and
so one imagines
Gertrude and Alice
taking Basket
for a walk. Even
Gisele unfolds her
tripod and we hear
the collapsing
rasp of her
immediate
shutter.

The fountain
of what we
imagine
must matter
years later
when we
are
alone.

WHATEVER THESE RUINS

I could drunk dial you
to tell you I am lonely
to tell you the love of my life
left years ago and I barely
remember tracing the soft
curve of her thigh
with thrumming
fingers. Could you tell
the truth from a lie?
If these are the gates
of hell, I will grab
their vined sides,
throw them wide. Open.
All thorns.

It's what you asked for.
To see the cut,
now clouded crystal,
the moth-worn dress,
the cake covered in mold.
Miss Havisham
has stopped painting her face. O
won't you come in?

Here, every kiss
is the same kiss,
contorted.

Abandoned bliss is
a faded portrait of your
face next to my face.

Always is as empty
as always—
but
the evening light
might transform us.

At the top
of the hill is a shadow
of something. Turn
away. Turn away.

CALL HER NAME

All of the stories would say just rest there in the moss, let it cover you like a blanket, like the care that never comes for you. All of the stories would say, fill your pockets with stones. The ones that line the shore to keep the ice from cracking the earth open like a geode. Walk into that spring-fed lake. Remember her letter: *I don't think two people could've been happier than we have been.* Call bullshit on that, perhaps, as Woolf, really, has been done to death. And because you're here. And they've torn down all the yellow wallpaper, all the walls around you. And everything is gone. Remember her letter: *I could never be another woman's lover.* That's the one. That's the one that turned you under. Because you broke so many times in her arms, and she brushed her lips through your hair, leaving her darkest mark. Call her needless. Call her ghosting. Call her from every parking lot you'd ever considered dying in. Again. And the vines of the roses climb your legs. They smell like a Hawthorne garden. Rapturous and full of poison. Call her name.

REMEDY

Once there was a clementine
when I couldn't speak

and a late afternoon on
the steps in the sun when

all I could do was think about
your hands so close to my hands.

And sometimes your voice
when no other voice mattered.

Some days we told stories
in sand and each granule was

a day I might put next to another
day until it didn't feel so much

like trying. Now every day
feels so much like trying.

When we first met, you said,
Why not get well?

And I believed you.
And then I didn't.

I woke up in the back of a car,
curled like a nautilus, the sound

of the sea ricocheting inside
my skull. But I was not an ocean.

I woke up in a cornfield and
the stars pleaded my defense,

but I was not a constellation
or a wanted galaxy. I woke up

in a hotel room, drenched
from days of pulled blinds

and constant doses I forgot to name,
as my own name slipped away.

I woke up and tried to go home.
But I wasn't available.

And neither was home.

I woke up and heard you say
that I couldn't possibly matter enough.

And I remembered then how important
it would always be to remain quiet.

I woke up and wrote every lie
I had ever been told. About god

and hope and the love of someone
coming to sit next to you

when you couldn't be more alone.
I woke up and walked away.

Because no one holds your hair back
when you are fresh out of brilliance.

Because there is no *well*.
Only *different*.

Heavenly

"She wants to have baked a cake that banishes sorrow, even if only for a little while. She wants to have produced something marvelous; something that would be marvelous even to those who do not love her." – *The Hours,* Michael Cunningham

I.
When the oven opens (such a slippery
gaping mouth and poetic history),
you'll see I've split apart,
a quite undone confection, center
of fresh cake batter. Slick sugar
and thick on delicate nail tips.

Dip in toes.   Tongue.   Come
into the sweetness. This
the most decadent of beaches
—a flush of heat   and skin, a salted
caramel in contrast.   Eyes lick
around the edges.

This too will run its course   (and kiss)
forgiveness falls
between us.

II.
And when I don't speak
And when I don't breathe
And you have in your lap
the most perfect pastry
won't it be lovely?   Won't it be electric!
That succulent meeting
of this world
and the next.

III.
Or this: Please stop calling me Sylvia &
I'll resist the urge to keep you as Clarissa.
You don't bake and I'm the better poet.
Under the umbrella, there is the tug of
you at my heart and the pull of the sky,
a fine unnamed veil of mist between us.
I am constantly reaching to touch you,
to tug you like a doll
from the shelf,
to make you remember.   The swing in the park

the stomp through the cemetery   the hours.
        Please remember   I went home and bought
stationery to write you a letter, to tell you I am well
again   to tell you I will stop drinking dinner.
I will run until the sadness ends.
I will lie awake at night,
after the endless asked-for fucking,
and say, of course, this is what the living do,
this is all ok.   To be alive is sacrifice.
It is not your death
that worries me.

A Remarkable Kind of Attention

I.
For every trick
or treater at the
door, I adjust
my height.
I hover
and remark
on a unique
costume detail
with sincere
delight. I believe
there is a kind
of bravery
in asking to be
seen. In asking
to be noticed
as magnificent.

II.
You believe
my favorite
candy type
is histrionic.
It leaves a nice
sour coating
on your tongue—
reminding you,
perhaps, that
on the day
I asked not
to die, you
closed
the door,
that crumpled
wrapper:

HELP ME
twisted, the last
in the bottom
of the bowl.

III.
At the end
of the film,
Bergman, in her
complete
genius, swears
she is simply
too mad
to save her
once-upon-
a-captor.
Sometimes
you take a knife
and turn your
back. No matter
how beautiful
those arms felt
and felt again
and once again
like ropes
around you.
When you
confuse candy
and safety.
When you
hear: *this*
reminded me
of you. But I
never actually
think of you. Because
why, why would

I turn to see
someone
who is always
half in
shadow?

IV.
The beauty
of knowing
where the
absence of
shimmer shows
a missing scale.
Where the blade
will fall the fastest.

How you will
look back at me
betrayed. How
you will cringe
at a certain kind
of laughter. Tell me
again, just
how much
you did (trick)
and didn't (treat)
love me.

V.
I looked you
in the eye
every single time.
And when I
pulled you in
like a delicate piece
of hand-spun

sugar, I felt
the molten
core of where
you began. And I
ended. It was,
in spite of you,
a remarkable
kind of attention.

CHRYSOPOEIA

i.
Cardamom and cinnamon
and orange zest
and eggs. Will you take
this church made
of cake?

ii.
The soft whoosh and clack
of contorting merino
from needle to needle.   Cast
to bind. My warmth
through your winter.

iii.
One is the serpent,
which has its poison
according to two compositions. *

iv.
If you
are beside me. I am.
Completing
the parting
of hands. Watch
as I spin you
to gold   to dust.

v.
You said: These words
are beautiful. I wish
I understood them.

vi.
Paint on canvas.
Brush to lips to forehead.
Circle.

*Cleopatra, Greek Egyptian alchemist, 3rd Century

AND THESE, MY LEAST BEST SELVES

the head, the heart, the shrink. the shrink's office. on her couch. in her arms.

Self #1

Head: First each leaf shredded from the philodendron vine, followed by a ritual gutting of the stuffed puppets.

Shrink: What do you want to talk about today?

Head: So many, so many mouthfuls of sand. Gritted teeth and decomposing jaw, I crawl the pale green walls like something damned.

Shrink: Sit with your feelings.

Head: Nails rake the leather from each couch cushion. Out of the corner of this post-historic eye, the glimmer of a small glass cat in a sand tray. *Mine*, I hiss, *meeeeeee.*

Shrink: Please, let me help you.

Head: And from my chest I wrench it free, this bludgeoned and silent heart, placing it gently, so gently at her feet.

Self #2

Head: And you said your prayers and played pretty things. Good girl, Alice. But you cry into your pillow nonetheless, flooding the room with the giant cups, spinning in thimbles and stars.

Heart: Mother, why have you left me here? Where they rip at my clothes and tear at my skin? I feel I will never be quite pretty again…

Head: and Tom Petty dances in. You are Alice made of cake. A cold slice from your abdomen smeared on slick and demented smiles. Every greedy bastard standing above you with a piece. And you look down with your giant Alice head and think,

Heart: Why, yes, it has come to this.

Head: A handful of lyrics and a shit-ton of weed. Never the straight teeth and starch they imagined for you, just the lunging guitars and phthalo blue. Devouring, this man in the shiny top hat. And so you say, as your body slips away, under tooth and under tongue,

Heart: Here's hoping the frosting is fine, you sad fucks. <3Alice

Self #3

Head: To live in the land of the missing. To hear a voice and not be able to listen or respond.

Shrink: Why are you fighting me?

Heart: I don't know.

Head: In the car I put my head on the steering wheel and scream. It is like this and it is not.

I am not the child in the doorway, tripping, tearing a hole in her knee on a loose nail. I am the child in the doorway, waiting, waiting, waiting. For no one.

Shrink: I love that little girl very much.

Head: Then I will protect her from you.

Heart: The child throws herself against the sky. No! Not this time!

Head: But you will get hurt. There are no more houses, warm fires, gentle caresses. There are no more inside places. There are no more chances. Or women to love.

Heart: Let her hold my hand.

Head: You should be quiet. You should want less. You can't stay with her.

There is only anger, ice white and flickering. Always underneath the calm.

Heart: I am in pain. And you aren't listening.

Head: I have taken care of you for so long.

Heart: You have ignored me.

Head: I have kept you safe.

Heart: You have kept me quiet.

Head: I have kept you quiet.

Heart: Let me talk to her.

Head: I am afraid of what you will say.

RESURRECTION

Why do we
love things that rise
and awaken? That lurch
fully formed and winged
from ashes
with only one wish:
to eat those
luscious brains?

Did you push
softpink
petals up
from the mud, delicate
lotus? (Yes, darling,
I know
you did. Come here,
let me kiss
it all better.)

Or did you roll
over, propped
up on an elbow
in your tranquil tomb
one morning and think,
Well. No. Shit—
today is not
a great day to be
dead?

It's ok,
we've all
been there.
Or have we? Will we?

There must be
a stained glass
story for this. Have I
mentioned that I am
not fond of crickets,
and I don't want
to have to return you—
so, please, be
on your way.

Maybe it's the against-
all-odds part,
that you could

be that. Sitting
right here next to me

on a bench in the sun
—every exit
and entrance,
every moment
of the crowd going wild
for you. Their moment
of belief making you
beautiful.

Hmmm, it could be
like that. Or you
were just late again.
In any case,
shake out the bottom
of your bag, will you?
I need
some gum.

PETITE ROUGE

I.

Not to forget or remember
but to undo. Put me to sleep
like all your fairytale girls.
And while I'm there bumbling
around in my sad nightgown,
unwind your voice from my ear,
your arms from my waist,
that last morsel of cake—poisoned
with shame. It was a long walk
with you lurking behind me in
the forest. There will be brambles
and briars and all sorts of shards.
As I sleep and as you pluck each piece
from my brain, count them all,
and count them back. Curse
as loudly as you want, I won't
hear you. And with each stab
and drip of remorse,
take my hand and take
yourself away.

II.

Now I am famous and
dead. Called Red and
collapsed in the belly
of all beautiful tales.
Immortal and sliced
like slivers of the best
foie gras. I ask you now,
who wouldn't
want me? Want me.

III.
Once upon a time,
I wore all my capes
for you. And with
every turn of the needle,
every small stitch,
I smiled, never realizing
I had linked my love
to thorns, to fangs.
So listen:
for every girl
in love with another,
there is always a wolf
and a dangerous path.
Choose wisely. Or wildly.
Or not at all.

ADDITIONAL DUTIES AS REQUIRED

She wanted to be
my mother
once. Upon
the dream
of lying
in her lap,
fingers threaded through
my thick
dark mane.
I told her
all my
secrets, and
we slept
entwined, satiated.
Divine.

Is it so wrong to kneel
at the altar of the exquisite?
To believe in the (un)holy breath
she blows against my neck,
as she says my name,
fingers that same spot
on the rosary. Poisons
the apple.
And kisses it all
wide open?

Sometimes
I just wanna
tear out
her gorgeous
old heart,
hold it gently in my snow
white hands, and watch it
stop feeling.

CAKE

It is always as close
as the next appointment
date and time written
on her seemingly innocuous
business card in her serial-
killer block-lettered scrawl,
so close I've lost the words
to catch the fear and send
it through the poetry sieve,
the ritual sifting of nouns
like flour, soda, baking
powder, salt. The wounds
have congealed, have already
become one enormous cake.

Each day I frost it
with a death so sweet,
I cannot even imagine inviting
my friends over to share.
They would not understand—
the color of it spectral, the taste
slivering into every bud of my tongue.
It is not painful. That is what I want
to make her understand. It is not painful
to lick this last bit of frosting
from my fingers.
                    Sometimes death
is not aligned with suffering.
Sometimes I am loved, am given
celebratory cake, and I still want an end,
that final swallowing. Sweet.
Like her intentions and her sighs
and all the frustrations we've swapped

and I've caused and can't,
can't take back what she knows.
She knows too much. I must
be very quiet now,
turn the poems down,
slide the last crumb
across my tongue.

ABOUT THE AUTHOR

Jen Rouse is the Director of the Center for Teaching and Learning at Cornell College. Her poems have appeared in *Poetry, Gulf Stream, Parentheses, Sinister Wisdom, Cleaver, Up the Staircase, Southern Florida Poetry Journal, Lavender Review,* and elsewhere. She was named a finalist for the Mississippi Review 2018 Prize Issue. Her chapbook, *Acid and Tender,* was a finalist for the Charlotte Mew Prize and published by Headmistress Press. The Poetry Annals published her micro chap, *Before Vanishing.* And *Riding with Anne Sexton,* Rouse's second chapbook is available from Bone & Ink Press in collaboration with dancing girl press. Find her at jen-rouse.com and on Twitter @jrouse.

Acknowledgments

Many thanks to the editors of the following publications, in which these poems appeared, sometimes in earlier versions:

A Restricted View From Under the Hedge: "Hummingbird Girl Gets Married," "When She Sings," "Additional Duties as Required"

Anti-Heroin Chic: "Whatever These Ruins"

BlazeVox: "An Afternoon in Paris"

Bombus: "Chrysopoeia"

Cleaver: "Remedy"

L'Éphémère Review: "Heavenly"

Rhythm and Bones: "And These, My Least Best Selves"

Southern Florida Poetry Journal: "Approaching"

The Ginger Collect: "Petite Rouge"

The Poetry Annals: "Cake"

HEADMISTRESS PRESS BOOKS

She/Her/Hers - Amy Lauren

Spoiled Meat - Nicole Santalucia

Cake - Jen Rouse

The Salt and the Song - Virginia Petrucci

mad girl's crush tweet - summer jade leavitt

Saturn coming out of its Retrograde - Briana Roldan

i am this girl - gina marie bernard

Week/End - Sarah Duncan

My Girl's Green Jacket - Mary Meriam

Nuts in Nutland - Mary Meriam, Hannah Barrett

Lovely - Lesléa Newman

Teeth & Teeth - Robin Reagler

How Distant the City - Freesia McKee

Shopgirls - Marissa Higgins

Riddle - Diane Fortney

When She Woke She Was an Open Field - Hilary Brown

God With Us - Amy Lauren

A Crown of Violets - Renée Vivien tr. Samantha Pious

Fireworks in the Graveyard - Joy Ladin

Social Dance - Carolyn Boll

The Force of Gratitude - Janice Gould

Spine - Sarah Caulfield

Diatribe from the Library - Farrell Greenwald Brenner

Blind Girl Grunt - Constance Merritt

Acid and Tender - Jen Rouse

Beautiful Machinery - Wendy DeGroat

Odd Mercy - Gail Thomas

The Great Scissor Hunt - Jessica K. Hylton

A Bracelet of Honeybees - Lynn Strongin

Whirlwind @ Lesbos - Risa Denenberg

The Body's Alphabet - Ann Tweedy

First name Barbie last name Doll - Maureen Bocka

Heaven to Me - Abe Louise Young

Sticky - Carter Steinmann

Tiger Laughs When You Push - Ruth Lehrer

Night Ringing - Laura Foley

Paper Cranes - Dinah Dietrich

On Loving a Saudi Girl - Carina Yun

The Burn Poems - Lynn Strongin

I Carry My Mother - Lesléa Newman

Distant Music - Joan Annsfire

The Awful Suicidal Swans - Flower Conroy

Joy Street - Laura Foley

Chiaroscuro Kisses - G.L. Morrison

The Lillian Trilogy - Mary Meriam

Lady of the Moon - Amy Lowell, Lillian Faderman, Mary Meriam

Irresistible Sonnets - ed. Mary Meriam

Lavender Review - ed. Mary Meriam

www.ingramcontent.com/pod-product-compliance
Lightning Source LLC
Chambersburg PA
CBHW072055040426

42447CB00012BB/3135